# SECRETS OF
# THE NATIONAL
# PARKS

# SECRETS OF
# THE NATIONAL
# PARKS

**WEIRD** and
**WONDERFUL FACTS**
about
**AMERICA'S NATURAL
WONDERS**

## AILEEN WEINTRAUB

STERLING CHILDREN'S BOOKS
New York

## STERLING CHILDREN'S BOOKS
New York

An Imprint of Sterling Publishing
1166 Avenue of the Americas
New York, NY 10036

The publisher has made every effort to ensure that the content of the book was current at the time of publication. It is always best to confirm information before making final travel plans, as information is always subject to change. The publisher cannot accept responsibility for any consequences arising from the use of this book.

ISBN 978-1-4549-2004-5

Distributed in Canada by Sterling Publishing Co., Inc.
c/o Canadian Manda Group, 664 Annette Street
Toronto, Ontario, Canada M6S 2C8
Distributed in the United Kingdom by GMC Distribution Services
Castle Place, 166 High Street, Lewes, East Sussex, England BN7 1XU

For information about custom editions, special sales, and premium and corporate purchases, please contact Sterling Special Sales at 800-805-5489 or specialsales@sterlingpublishing.com.

Manufactured in China
Lot #:
2  4  6  8  10  9  7  5  3  1
08/16

www.sterlingpublishing.com

Original illustrations by Jane Sanders

# CONTENTS

# INTRODUCTION

In the United States, people visit national parks to play, explore, and learn. They also come to enjoy nature! With 59 parks to choose from, there is so much to do and see. Hiking, climbing, fishing, and relaxing are all part of the fun. The great thing about national parks is that even if you've already visited a park, there is always something new to discover.

In *Secrets of the National Parks* we've dug a little deeper to find

out what really makes the parks so special. In this book, you'll read about tales of survival, underground gems, hidden views, and much more. This way, when you visit a national park you'll have all the details, facts, and tidbits to make your trip even more exciting! Are you ready to hit the trail? Let's go! Turn the page to find out cool secrets about the U.S. national parks!

# HISTORY UNCOVERED

The **symbol** of the National Park Service is the **arrowhead**. If you look closely at the arrowhead, you will see a sequoia tree, a bison, mountains, and water. This shows all the different reasons to visit a National Park.

In 1872, Yellowstone became the first national park in the country. Thirty-one years later, park officials wanted to build an arch at the north entrance of the park. At the same time, President Theodore Roosevelt planned a two-week visit. He had the honor of laying the very first cornerstone. Park officials decided to name the new entrance Roosevelt Arch.

The **Roosevelt Arch** is 50 feet high and has a tower on each side. It was designed to allow horse-drawn carriages to pass through the park. On the **top of the arch**, there is a quote. It reads: "For the Benefit and Enjoyment of the People." These words soon became the **unofficial motto** for all national parks.

The national parks are full of amazing history. Check out some National Park firsts.

The first park to have a woman ranger: **Yosemite, California**

★ ★ ★

The first cave to become a park: **Wind Cave, South Dakota**

★ ★ ★

The first park printed on a National Park quarter: **Hot Springs, Arkansas**

★ ★ ★

The first park named after a U.S. president: **Theodore Roosevelt National Park, North Dakota**

John Muir was one of the first people to help **create** the national parks. He was a writer who really enjoyed America's **wilderness**. He loved nature so much that in 1890 he and others created a national park. That park was **Yosemite**. After that, he helped create four more parks.

People have been living at Rocky Mountain National Park in Colorado for over 10,000 years! Scientists have found **artifacts** from **prehistoric humans** all throughout the park. Arrowheads and stone walls used to trap animals are just some of the **ancient finds**.

QUICK

QUIZ

In 1872, land was set aside to create Yellowstone National Park. Can you guess which U.S. president helped create the park?

**a)** Abraham Lincoln

**b)** Theodore Roosevelt

**c)** Ulysses S. Grant

**d)** George Washington

Answer: c

When you think of national parks, the last thing you might think about is a **rocket launching base**. But that is exactly what you will find in **Everglades National Park** in Florida. Stop by the visitor's center to take a tour of the Nike Missile Site. In 1964, it was set up to defend the United States from attacks. You'll also see soldiers' sleeping quarters, guard-dog kennels, and a control center.

Staying in a hotel might be fun, but it's even more fun to stay with a **local family**. The National Park of American Samoa has a special program called **Homestay**. You can live with a Samoan family in their house in the rainforest. They'll teach you all about **village customs**. You'll even get to try activities such as weaving mats with dried tree leaves.

Every park is unique. Check out the facts below to see what makes the national parks so special.

The only park that . . .

. . . is patrolled by dogs:
**Denali National Park & Preserve, Alaska**

★ ★ ★

. . . is south of the equator:
**National Park of American Samoa, South Pacific**

★ ★ ★

. . . keeps growing because its volcanoes are getting bigger:
**Hawaii Volcanoes National Park, Hawaii**

. . . is made up almost completely of water:

**Voyageurs National Park, Minnesota**

★ ★ ★

. . . . has hottest temperature on record [134 degrees!]:

**Furnace Creek—Death Valley National Park, California**

★ ★ ★

. . . . has the most rainfall:

**Olympic National Park, Washington**.

# QUICK QUIZ

*Mako sica* is the name the Lakota people used for the land that is now Theodore Roosevelt National Park in North Dakota. It means "badlands." Can you guess why? Here's a hint: This park is sometimes compared to the surface of the moon.

**a)** The land was rocky, bare, and dry.

**b)** The land misbehaved.

**c)** The land was mean.

**d)** The land was near an ocean.

Answer: a

Everybody knows that Yellowstone was the first national park, but some people say that's not fair. They think the honor should go to Hot Springs National Park in Arkansas. That's because Hot Springs was the first land that Congress agreed to protect in the entire country! That happened in 1832, but the land didn't become an official park until 1921.

ON THE
TRAIL

"Explore, Learn, and Protect!" That's the **motto** for all **Junior Rangers**. As a JR, you get to do fun activities, speak to rangers, and get your very own **badge**. Next time you're at a national park, stop in at the visitor's center and sign up!

Ever think about hiking all the trails in the national parks? It would be impossible! If you placed all the trails from end to end, they would stretch 18,000 miles. That's like walking from New York to California and back three times! Plus, some of the trails are water, which would be impossible to cross on foot!

You're not afraid of **ghosts**, are you? If you are, you'd better stay away from **Lulu City** at Rocky Mountain National Park in Colorado. This is an **abandoned ghost town**! If you're brave, you can explore the old cabins where miners lived over a hundred years ago.

When you think of national parks, you think of wide open space. But some parks are bigger than others. Most of the biggest national parks are in Alaska!

### 1.
Wrangell–St. Elias National Park, Alaska

**13,188,000 acres**

### 2.
Gates of the Arctic National Park, Alaska

**8,500,000 acres**

### 3.
Denali National Park, Alaska

**4,740,911 acres**

### 4.
Katmai National Park, Alaska

**4,021,327 acres**

### 5.
Death Valley National Park, California/ Nevada

**3,372,401 acres**

## 6.
### Glacier Bay National Park, Alaska
**3,224,320 acres**

## 7.
### Lake Clark National Park, Alaska
**2,619,520 acres**

## 8.
### Yellowstone National Park, Wyoming/ Idaho/Montana
**2,219,790 acres**

## 9.
### Kobuk Valley National Park, Alaska
**1,750,400 acres**

## 10.
### Everglades National Park, Florida
**1,508,537 acres**

QUICK
QUIZ

Many states have more than one national park. But there is one state that has more than any other. This state has nine parks. Can you guess which state it is?

**a)** New York

**b)** Alaska

**c)** California

**d)** Oregon

Answer: c

Check out the 3,000-year-old **rock paintings** at Arches National Park in Utah. To find them, just follow the stream to the Lower Courthouse Wash trail. At the stream crossings along the way, look closely in the sand. You may see **animal tracks** belonging to bighorn sheep, beavers, coyotes, and maybe even mountain lions.

Love **extreme sports**?
If so, there's no better
place to visit than **Joshua
Tree National Park**
in California. This park has
8,000 **climbing routes**!
Rock climbing is one of
the best ways to see great
boulders up close. It is also
a good way to test your
strength. You can sign up
for lessons at one of the
climbing stores near
the park.

Yosemite National Park in California can be a crowded place. For a quieter experience, take the 13-mile Valley Floor Loop to see **boulders**, **cliffs**, and **waterfalls**. The trail was washed out years ago. Since then, most people have forgotten about it.

Skiing is a fun sport—how would you like to try it on sand? That's exactly what you can do at Great Sand Dunes National Park in Colorado. The sand dunes are over 12,000 years old. If skiing is not your thing, don't worry. You can also sled or slide down the dunes. While you're there, don't forget to build a sandcastle!

QUICK
QUIZ

Taking care of a national park is hard work. That's why volunteers are so important. They do everything from clearing trails to talking with visitors. Some collect information about plants and animals. Can you guess how many volunteers work in the parks each year?

**a)** 21,000

**b)** 100

**c)** 1 million

**d)** 221,000

Answer: d

Some of the greatest record breakers in the country or world happen in national parks. Check out these natural chart toppers.

At **20,310 feet**, Denali is the tallest mountain in North America. (Denali National Park, Alaska)

★ ★ ★

At **1,604 feet**, Lechuguilla cave is the deepest cave in the United States. (Carlsbad Caverns National Park, New Mexico)

★ ★ ★

At **282 feet** below sea level, Badwater Basin is the lowest point in North America. (Death Valley National Park, California)

At **1,932 feet**, Crater Lake is the deepest lake in North America. (Crater Lake National Park, Oregon)

★ ★ ★

At **750 feet**, Star Dune is the highest sand dune. (Great Sand Dunes National Park, Colorado)

★ ★ ★

At **700 square miles**, the Harding ice field is the biggest ice field. (Kenai Fjords National Park, Alaska)

At Great Smoky Mountains National Park in North Carolina and Tennessee, you can become a citizen scientist. These helpers gather information about the park. You might be asked to study flowers, watch birds, or even catch butterflies. To sign up, go to the Great Smoky Mountains Institute at Tremont.

There are 17 **carriage road bridges** in Acadia National Park in Maine. Each one has its own **unique design**. To find the only bridge in the park that is made of cobblestones, look for the Jordon Stream Trail. On the way, you'll find other cool bridges too. You'll also be treated to a view of two hills named The Bubbles.

WILD
WOODLANDS

Can you imagine a tree **taller** than a **skyscraper**? Head over to the Giant Forest in Sequoia National Park in California. Here you'll find over 8,000 huge **sequoia trees**. They are the world's **largest** and **longest-living** trees.

The **largest** living tree in the entire world lives in the Giant Forest of Sequoia National Park. The tree even has its **own** name! It's known as General Sherman.

Height: **274 feet** tall

★ ★ ★

Width: **102.6 feet** around the base

★ ★ ★

Weight: **2.7 million** pounds

Largest branch: **6.8 feet**

★ ★ ★

Age: **2,100 years old**

★ ★ ★

The General Sherman tree is named
after the famous Civil War hero
General William Tecumseh Sherman.
Even though General Sherman
is the largest tree in the world,
it is not the tallest.

Would you believe there's a tree that you can **drive right through**? It can be found across Crescent Meadow Road in Sequoia & Kings Canyon National Parks in California. When it fell in 1937, it was believed to be 2,000 years old. Instead of removing it, rangers made a **passageway**. It's called the Tunnel Log passage.

Sequoias are the **largest trees**, but redwood trees are the **tallest**. You'll find plenty of them in Redwood National and State Parks in California. When you're done looking up, make sure to search for **pinecones** on the ground. For such large trees, a redwood's pinecones can be **teeny tiny**. Some pinecones are about the size of **grapes**!

Even though redwoods are huge trees, they have shallow roots. They reach only 6 to 12 feet into the earth. So how do they live for thousands of years without falling over? Their roots can stretch out over 100 feet from their trunk. Sometimes they even grab onto other tree roots for more support. That's how they stand up to wind and floods.

**QUICK QUIZ**

**How long have redwood trees been around?**

**a)** 1 million years

**b)** 2,000 years

**c)** 240 million years

**d)** 10,000 years

Redwoods are often confused with sequoias, but they are not the same at all. They are close cousins! Here are some interesting facts about redwoods.

Where you'll find them:
**along the coast**

★ ★ ★

How tall they can grow:
**378 feet high**

★ ★ ★

How long they can live:
**2,000 years**

How thick their bark grows:
**up to 12 inches**

★ ★ ★

How wide around they are:
**up to 20 feet**

★ ★ ★

How long it takes to grow from
seed to 100 feet:
**50 years!**

Ready, Set, Action! Redwood trees are so **special** that they've been **filmed** in **famous movies**. Scenes from *Star Wars 6* and *Jurassic Park* were shot at Redwood National and State Parks in California.

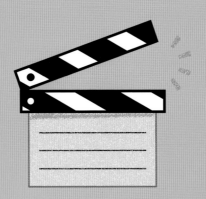

You've heard of traffic jams, but do you know about logjams? The Petrified Forest National Park in Arizona is filled with fossilized trees. If you head to the Long Logs Trail, you'll find a prehistoric logjam. That's where the trees got backed up in an ancient stream. Some of the logs are over 100 feet long!

QUICK
QUIZ

**The Petrified Forest is part of
a desert that Spanish explorers
named. The explorers named the
desert after the beautiful colors
they saw in the sand. Can you guess
what this desert is called?**

**a)** The Red Desert

**b)** The Painted Desert

**c)** The Boring Desert

**d)** The Colorful Desert

Answer: b

Big Bend National Park in Texas is **hot**, **dry**, and **far** from major roads. That means that desert plants love it! There are over 40 kinds of **cacti** growing there. That's more than any other national park! Some of them have interesting names like **horse crippler**, **eagle claw**, and **strawberry hedgehog**. April is the best time to see them bloom.

Take a **stroll** through Saguaro National Park in Arizona to see 45-foot-tall cacti. Saguaros (pronounced *sah-wah-rohs*) are the **tallest cacti** on Earth. They grow less than 1 inch every 8 years! If you're lucky, you might see a **crested saguaro**. These spread out like a fan instead of growing straight. Only 25 of them have been found in the park.

There is only one place in the whole world where the silversword plant grows. You'll have to climb the Haleakalā Volcano in Hawaii to see it. These plants have silver "hairs" that puff out around the bottom. When they are older, they shoot up a stalk that has roughly 600 flower heads.

Denali National Park is a place of extreme temperatures. This means that plants have to be hardy. In cooler spots, you might find lichen, mosses, and fungi. In the short summer season, search for bluebells, goldenrod, and forget-me-nots. Look carefully. You can find more than 650 different types of flowering plants.

Are you a **leaf-peeper**? You are if you like to see the **fall colors** change. A fun way to enjoy the **leaves** is to saddle up! Great Smoky Mountains National Park has 500 miles of horseback riding trails. You can bring your own horse, or join a tour.

# NATURAL SURPRISES

Put on your **winter gear** and visit Kenai Fjords National Park in Alaska. This park is covered in snow and ice. Here, the glaciers are always **moving** and **changing**. One of the park's major attractions, Exit Glacier, has retreated an average of 30 feet per year between 1973 and 2013.

Looking for a chilling adventure? Head to Wrangell-St. Elias National Park in Alaska to see over 150 glaciers. One of them is called Malaspina. It is bigger than the entire state of Rhode Island!

The best way to see a glacier **up close** is to take a **private plane ride** through Wrangel-St. Elias. Sometimes the pilot will drop you off and let you walk around on the glacier! These tours are called **flightseeing tours** because you get to see so much while you're flying. You can find out all about them at the park's visitor center.

If you want to see one of
the 25 active glaciers
at Glacier National Park
in Montana, you'd better
hurry. Scientists say that
by 2030, these glaciers
will have melted away.
Many of them have already
disappeared. There used to
be 150!

# Word Search

In Glacier National Park, you'll find more than just ice. Circle the words below to see what else you'll find.

```
X V V R B Y G P B R V I K G P
E A L D C R K Q W Y B L I C S
G K B H W G A H G B W C A W S
J C Z Z G T S F O B E R O T E
S R E W O L F D L I W D V B H
W W T J Y S Z N K X A V B T S
S A E I B Q C Y C E D D U X R
X E T Q A B W M M M G Y P M A
M X K E C B Q V J K K M P H M
H G I A R G Z X R N U D G J S
W T B J L F C R J G A G Z P R
G O A T S T A M K H U J D S E
J J M R O Y J L P E E H S N J
R D J U G D N G L K H E Z O M
O F O T U P P Q Q S X L Y W M
```

Goats     Marshes     Meadows     Snow

Lakes     Waterfalls     Sheep     Wildflowers

Check the answer key on page 158 to see the completed word search.

Beneath Yellowstone National Park lies a **supervolcano**. This is a type of volcano that has a **gigantic eruption**. Not to worry. The last time Yellowstone had an enormous eruption was **640,000 years ago**. Scientists think that it will be at least another 10,000 years before it erupts again!

Devil's Kitchen in Lassen Volcanic National Park in California is a nail-biting trail. The steam hisses beneath the ground. Mud boils all around. And it smells like rotten eggs! One step off the trail and you can sink your foot into superhot mud.

QUICK
**QUIZ**

**If it's hot lava and big plumes of smoke you're looking for, there is one place you are sure to find it. This park is home to two of the most active volcanoes in the world: Kilauea and Mauna Loa. Can you guess the park?**

**a)** Hawai'i Volcanoes

**b)** Yellowstone

**c)** Zion

**d)** Denali

Answer: a

Mount Rainer is a **volcano** in Mount Rainier National Park in Washington. Every year, over 10,000 people try to **climb** to the top. Most of those people never make it all the way up. It's just too hard! Only about 2,500 people reach the **summit** each year.

Crater Lake in Crater Lake National Park in Oregon is a **caldera**. This means that it's really just a **huge hole** that was made when a volcano **collapsed** about 7,500 years ago. Over time, the hole filled with rain and snow. Now it's a lake that holds up to 5 trillion gallons of water!

Names such as Devils Garden, Dark Angel, and Devil Dog Spire sound like **scary movies**. They're really the names of the **arches** at Arches National Park in Utah. This park has over 2,000 natural sandstone arches that were made **millions of years ago**! As you stroll through the park, see if the arches look anything like their names.

QUICK
QUIZ

At Bryce Canyon National Park in Utah, erosion has made an unusual landscape. Tall, thin rock formations cover the park. Some are as tall as a human being, and others are taller than the biggest skyscrapers. Can you guess what these formations are called?

**a)** bunnies

**b)** hoodoos

**c)** boodoos

**d)** panthers

Answer: b

Geysers are hot springs that boil up and then shoot steam straight into the air. Yellowstone National Park has about 300 geysers. The most famous one is Old Faithful.

The number of times Old Faithful has erupted since Yellowstone became a national park: **1 million and counting**

★ ★ ★

Average time between eruptions: **92 minutes**

★ ★ ★

Height that steam shoots from the geyser: **from 90 to 184 feet**

Average temperature of the steam: **about 350 degrees Fahrenheit**

★ ★ ★

Duration of each eruption: **between 1 and 5 minutes**

★ ★ ★

Average number of eruptions a day: **17 times**

★ ★ ★

Amount of water in each eruption: **3,700 to 8,400 gallons**

**Old Faithful** is a **geyser** that erupts more than any of the other large geysers in Yellowstone. Want to see it **erupt** right now? You can check out Old Faithful's **webcam**. Go to https://www.nps.gov/features/yell/webcam/oldFaithfulStreaming.html to see Old Faithful in action.

When Yellowstone opened, people didn't know how to **behave** at a park. Some people put **laundry soap** in the geysers. Others threw in **wood** and **big logs**. They wanted to see what would happen when the geysers **erupted**. Since then, we have learned not to disturb nature.

# SECRET
# LOOKOUTS

Not many parks have a **railroad**  running through them, but Ohio's Cuyahoga Valley National Park does! Hop aboard the **old-fashioned steam engine** for a grand tour. You'll ride through marshlands, floodplains, and steep valley walls. You'll also get to see some pretty interesting **wildlife**, such as beavers, muskrats, and minks. You can even have dinner on board the train!

Take a two-hour tram tour through Shark Valley in Florida's Everglades National Park. This open-air bus will cruise by alligators, red-bellied turtles, and racer snakes. Halfway through the tour, you can climb a tower for a bird's-eye view of the Everglades. Find the tour at the Shark Valley Visitor Center.

Sightsee on the Red Jammers in Glacier National Park. These **old buses** will give you an idea of what it was like to **travel** around the park in the 1930s. Long ago, the drivers used to have to **jam the gears** as they drove along the winding roads. That's how the buses got their name!

QUICK
QUIZ

When people talk about "landscape" they are talking about the scenery or view. When it comes to national parks, there is a lot of fun stuff to hear too. Can you guess the word for this?

**a)** hearingscape

**b)** soundscape

**c)** earscape

**d)** listenscape

Answer: b

Many people had to give up their homes to create the Great Smoky Mountains National Park in the 1930s. These people left behind houses, barns, and churches. Over 90 buildings have been preserved for visitors. Just pick up an auto tour guide at the visitor's center. You'll discover what life was like before the park was built.

Get an up-close look at the gray whale migration. It happens every year from December through mid-March at Channel Islands National Park in California. Hike up the short trail to Cavern Point. Then, look out from the hill above Scorpion Anchorage. You'll have a whale of a time!

Take a **hike** on the Bristlecone and Glacier trail at Great Basin National Park in Nevada. You'll be treated to a **view** of 5,000-year-old trees called **bristlecone pines**. At the end of the trail, you'll see one of the only glaciers in Nevada. Look closely to see ice sliding very slowly down the **giant boulders**.

Each year, **281 million** people head to a national park. Check out the parks that have the most visitors.

More than **10 million** people visit the Great Smoky Mountains. That is twice as much as any other park.

★ ★ ★

Over **4.8 million** people come to see the Grand Canyon. That's because it's one of the largest canyons in the world.

★ ★ ★

**4 million** visitors go to Yosemite. The Yosemite Valley was carved out by glaciers millions of years ago. Now there are huge cliffs and giant waterfalls.

Over **3.5 million** people visit Yellowstone. There is certainly a lot to see. The park spans three states: Wyoming, Montana, and Idaho.

\* \* \*

Over **3.4 million** people head to Rocky Mountain National Park. This park has 67 different kinds of large mammals, over 280 types of birds, and 11 different kinds of fish. It even has an area just for butterflies!

Shenandoah National Park in Virginia has over 75 **lookout points** along Skyline Drive. This **winding road** stretches 105 miles and overlooks the Blue Ridge Mountains. It's the perfect place to see the **fall colors** change. Want more adventure? The park has over 500 miles of hiking trails to explore.

For the **best view** of the **Smoky Mountains**, climb to the top of the tower at Clingmans Dome. At 6,643 feet, it's the **highest spot** in the park. It's also the **highest point** in the state of Tennessee! On clear days, you can see up to 100 miles.

There's nothing like waking up early and heading out to watch the sunrise. Here are some of the most breathtaking places worth getting out of bed for.

Cadillac Mountain in Acadia National Park is **1,530 feet** high. From October through March of each year, it is the first place in the country to view the sunrise.

Watch the sunrise from the top of a **volcano**. Head over to Haleakalā National Park in Hawaii. You can even rent bikes to ride down the volcano after the sun rises.

★ ★ ★

Many people believe that one of the best places in the entire world to see the sunrise is at the **Grand Canyon's South Rim**.

When you go to **Theodore Roosevelt National Park** in North Dakota, plan your visit around the night sky. You'll get a crystal-clear view of the **Milky Way, planets**, and **stars**. The sky is superdark because there is almost no light pollution here. You'll find special night-viewing areas around the park. If you're really lucky, you might even see the northern lights.

Bryce Canyon National Park is a great place for **stargazers**. Look up at the sky **after sundown** and you'll be in for a treat. On a clear night, you can see 7,500 stars! That's way more stars than what you might see anywhere else on the continent.

Want to watch wildlife in action? Then take a sleigh ride on the National Elk Refuge in the Jackson Hole area in Wyoming. A horse will pull you in a giant sleigh across the snow. You'll see thousands of elk up close. You can get tickets at the Jackson Hole and Greater Yellowstone visitors' center.

**Grand Teton National Park** in Wyoming is one of the only places in the country where you can still see **wild bison** roaming the range. One good place to look for them is Antelope Flats Road on the **east side of the park**. These animals weigh up to 2,000 pounds and can run as fast as 40 miles per hour.

If you're lucky, you might catch a glimpse of the **pronghorn antelope** while visiting Grand Teton. These **superfast animals** can run more than 50 miles per hour through grassland! They are the fastest animals in North America. They migrate farther than any other mammal does.

Tag along on the **llama train** at Great Smoky Mountains National Park. Three days a week llamas **carry supplies** up to a lodge in the park. To see them, head to the Trillium Gap trail before 8:00 am from March to November. Just don't stand downwind of the llamas! They're **stinky**!

**QUICK QUIZ**

**Great Smoky Mountains is known as the Salamander Capital of the World. There are so many salamanders in the park that they outnumber visitors. Most of the salamanders that live here don't have lungs. Can you guess how they breathe?**

**a)** through their claws

**b)** through their skin

**c)** through their eyes

**d)** through their neck

Answer: b

Did you know that lobsters smell with the hair on their legs and their antennae? Sign up for a **lobster boat tour** at Acadia National Park to find out all sorts of **fun facts** about lobsters. On the Lulu Lobster Boat, the captain will tell you all about **lobster boxing**. You'll also learn about the life cycle of a lobster. You may even get to see how a lobster trap works.

Canine Rangers **patrol** over 3,000 miles of Denali National Park. Head to the park in summer to see these **sled dogs** in action. First the **huskies** are hitched to a sled. Then they run along a track around their kennels.

These animals listed below are in danger of becoming extinct. Luckily, the national parks are doing everything they can to help increase their population.

- **Black-footed ferret**—Badlands National Park and Wind Cave National Park

- **Sawfish**—Biscayne National Park

- **Mist forest stonefly**—Glacier National Park

- **Sierra Nevada yellow-legged frog**—Yosemite National Park

- **American pika**—Rocky Mountain National Park

Bighorn sheep can be found **hanging out** on the rocky cliffs of Yellowstone. These **daredevils** like to **jump** from ledge to ledge! One way to tell if you're looking at a male or female is to notice the sheep's **horns**. The males have thick curled horns, and females have smaller, thin horns.

Not all parks have **mascots**, but Glacier National Park does! Its mascot is a **mountain goat**. These goats have **big hooves** to help them keep their balance on steep mountain slopes. They can jump up to 12 feet at a time! To see them, head over to Goat Lick Overlook. This is where the goats lick **natural minerals** from the rocks.

Like music? How about
a frog concert?
Go to Shark Valley in
the Everglades after a
rainstorm. Listen carefully,
and you might hear the
sound of tree frogs,
cricket frogs, and oak
toads. You'll be treated to
a whole symphony!

QUICK
QUIZ

The island scrub jay is one of the rarest birds in the world. It has bright blue feathers and makes a loud screeching sound. You'll only find this special bird hiding out in one national park. Can you guess which one?

**a)** Channel Islands

**b)** Yosemite

**c)** Joshua Tree

**d)** Yellowstone

Answer: a

When you're in Pinnacles National Park in California, make sure to **look up** at the sky. You might spot the **largest flying bird** in North America! This rare bird is called the **condor**. Once, there were only 22 condors in California. Scientists bred them to make sure they didn't become extinct. If you see one, look at the bird's head. The skin **changes** from **yellow** to **red**!

# WATER
## DISCOVERIES

Love water? Imagine visiting a national park **without ever touching land**. You can rent a **houseboat** at Voyageurs National Park in Minnesota. There are four lakes to choose from: Rainy Lake, Kabetogama Lake, Namakan Lake, and Sand Point Lake.

There are over 200 **shipwrecks** in the waters of Dry Tortugas National Park in Florida! Beginning in 1513, the Spanish shipped **coffee**, **meat**, and **cotton** in return for **gold**. Hurricanes, shallow waters, and strong currents wiped out many ships. It was a **dangerous** route. Today, scuba divers can swim through this underwater history.

QUICK
QUIZ

The Cuyahoga Valley National
Park in Ohio gets its name from a
Mohawk Native American word. Can
you guess what "Cuyahoga" means?
Hint: A 22-mile river winds through
the park.

**a)** deep sand    **b)** high mountain

**c)** dark cave    **d)** crooked river

Answer: d

Schoodic Head in Acadia is a great place to **watch the waves**. At 440 feet, this spot is the **highest point** in the park. If you look closely at the **granite rocks** below, you'll see solid black strips. This is **magma** that forced its way through the rock and then hardened!

The **Ship Harbor Trail** in Acadia is an easy loop that will take you along the shore of Mount Desert Island. Here you can find **tide pools** filled with **sea life**. Look for whelks, mussels, sea urchins, sea stars, and barnacles.

# Word Search

Circle all the water sports you can
do at Acadia National Park.

```
X J B A V H M Q S X G Q S X J
B M S T U W F T S S O Z G U E
K L A J K S R F W X O H M M Q
Y H Z O B J S U N S X R M T K
W C O H Q X E O K N W R Z G Q
C G N I L I A S Y O L D C N F
C A B D V K A P O R X N Q I I
G E N K A F V S G K K I Q F C
D N I O S Q B U N E H X D R W
N I I L E L U T I L Z I W U J
O O V K M I U Z M I O A W S R
S R P I A W N M M N V X Q D H
X V A F N Y G G I G R J W Q X
S Z X C C G A C W D H I J W T
F I S H I N G K S J I Y A I K
```

Canoeing    Fishing    Sailing    Surfing

Diving    Kayaking    Snorkeling    Swimming

Check the answer key on page 158
to see the completed word search.

Get an up-close view of 950 types of fish. In **American Samoa** you can go **snorkeling** off the coast of Ofu Island. You'll come face to face with **sea creatures** such as barracuda, the blacktip reef shark, and maybe even a sea turtle. You'll also see more than 250 types of **colorful coral**.
Get your snorkel gear ready!

Want to see some of the coolest waterfalls in the country? You'll find them at Great Smoky Mountains National Park. Over **9.4 million** visitors headed to this park in 2013 to see the falls.

The tallest waterfall in the park:
**100-foot-high** Ramsey Falls

★ ★ ★

The waterfall named for a Cherokee chief:
**20-foot-high** Abrams Falls

★ ★ ★

The only waterfall you can stand behind:
**25-foot-high** Grotto Falls

The falls where you'll see a rainbow
on a sunny day:
**80-foot-high** Rainbow Falls

★ ★ ★

The waterfall that freezes into an
icy column in winter:
**90-foot-high** Hen Wallows Falls

★ ★ ★

The waterfall that has a
walkway dividing its upper
and lower sections:
**80-foot-high** Laurel Falls

The **smallest park** in the country is Hot Springs National Park in Arkansas. It is only 5,500 acres. People come here to **soak** in one of the 47 **hot springs**. The temperature in these pools reaches to 143 degrees Fahrenheit!

The hot springs at Hot Springs National Park didn't just appear. They started out as rainwater over 4,000 years ago. The water sunk a mile into the earth. It heated up underground and bubbled to the surface.

# CLOSE CALLS

Ever wonder how Death Valley National Park in California got its creepy name? In 1849, a bunch of men looking for gold went missing. It was during the Gold Rush and they were trying to find a shortcut. The men were convinced the valley would be their grave. When they were finally rescued, one man looked back and said, "Good-bye, Death Valley."

In 1869, adventurer John Wesley Powell and nine other men **rafted** the **wild rapids** of the Grand Canyon in Arizona. The men **traveled** 1,000 miles in three months. It was a **dangerous trip**. They lost one boat and most of their supplies in the river. Only seven of the men survived the trip.

In 1914 three **hikers climbed** Lassen Volcanic National Park in California. As they were climbing, the volcano **erupted**. Two of the hikers made it down. The third got **knocked out** from the explosion. When he woke up, he saw the lava all around him. All three men survived the blast.

QUICK
QUIZ

When the parks first opened, people had a lot to learn about nature. Sometimes people got too close to the wild animals. In some parks, viewing stands were even set up to watch wildlife. Can you guess why?

**a)** To watch birds make nests

**b)** To watch penguins fish

**c)** To watch bears eat from dumpsters

**d)** To watch people have lunch

Answer: c

People have to share the park with bears. Usually, bears will leave you alone or run away. Most of the time, they won't attack. Here are some tips to stay safe:

- Hike with three or more people.
- Be aware of what's around you.
- Don't sneak up on animals.
- Make a lot of noise so animals aren't surprised.
- Carry bear spray.
- Don't run if you see a bear.
- Stay on paths and trails.
- Always pack up your food and put it away when you are done.

Long ago, people used to be allowed to fish in the waters around **Fishing Cone geyser** in Yellowstone. Once, a man **accidentally dropped** the fish he caught into the geyser. He thought it was lost forever. Moments later, the fish **floated** to the top. It had been **boiled** and was ready to eat!

Park rangers have a **hard job**. Some have it harder than others. Ranger Roy Sullivan worked at Shenandoah National Park in Virginia from 1942 to 1977. During that time, he was **struck by lightning** seven times! Luckily, he lived to tell about it each time.

The Enchanted Valley Chalet is a **historical guest house** at Olympic National Park in Washington. The house isn't used anymore, but many people still **enjoy visiting**. Until recently the entire house was in danger of falling into the river! Plans were made to save the house. It was moved 100 feet.

Zion National Park in Utah is known for gigantic rockslides. Thousands of years ago, one of the biggest rockslides in history took place. When the rocks fell, they made a hole so big it was over 200 feet deep. That hole is now Sentinel Lake.

SLIDE AREA

Did you know that forest fires are good for trees and plants? They help them grow! Check out these facts about forest fires in Yellowstone National Park.

Fires burn the strongest during the **midafternoon**.

★ ★ ★

Most fires at Yellowstone are reported at **3:03 p.m.**

★ ★ ★

Fires have been happening at Yellowstone for more than **14,000 years**.

There have been up to 78 fires
a year at Yellowstone.

★ ★ ★

The most fires happen between
June and September.

★ ★ ★

About 25 fires a year
start because of
lightning strikes.

Miners Castle is a famous **rock formation** in Pictured Rocks National Lakeshore in Michigan. In 2006, most of the rock fell into Lake Superior! A **fisherman** saw the whole thing crumble. These rockfalls happen when huge rocks **warm up** after a long winter. This was the fifth major rockfall in recent history. Luckily, no one was hurt.

In 2015, Kevin Jorgeson and Tommy Caldwell were the first to **free-climb** the largest block of granite in the world. This **huge rock** is called El Capitan and can be found at Yosemite National Park. The climbers used only their **hands and feet** and a safety rope. It took 19 days. Jorgeson fell 11 times! They made rock-climbing history.

# UNDERGROUND MYSTERIES

Beware! In Yellowstone National Park there is a **cave** with a **serpent's tongue**. It's called Dragon's Mouth Spring. When **gases** rise up from the ground, it causes water to splash against the cave walls. The "tongue" is really the **hot steam** shooting out of the cave's entrance. If you listen carefully, you'll hear the belly of the dragon rumbling.

Find your **inner caveman**. At Sequoia & Kings Canyon you can check out a **real bat cave**. The Bat Grotto in Boyden Cavern is open for tours all summer long. Just don't wake the bats. They sleep all day!

## QUICK QUIZ

**Guess how fast a Brazilian free-tailed bat can fly?**

**a)** 25 miles per hour (as fast as a champion bicyclist)

**b)** 65 miles per hour (as fast as a car on the highway)

**c)** 700 miles per hour (as fast as an airplane)

**d)** 150 miles per hour (as fast as a train)

Answer: a

Thinking about **kayaking** through the sea caves at Channel Islands National Park? You might have some **unexpected company**. Harbor seals like to swim alongside kayaks outside the caves. Inside the cave, look over your head for **crusty barnacles**. And don't forget your headlamp!

# Word Search

**Find the animals that live in the caves of Carlsbad Caverns.**

```
C  K  M  Q  Y  Z  G  T  L  A  T  A  T  S  E
N  E  S  I  L  V  E  R  F  I  S  H  W  F  R
C  U  N  J  R  S  T  R  P  L  G  A  J  Y  L
N  R  V  T  D  Q  C  C  M  I  L  W  N  O  F
X  L  I  X  I  B  A  G  Y  L  V  S  J  P  F
F  Y  Z  C  W  P  D  B  O  M  P  G  R  K  R
B  H  U  D  K  H  E  W  C  I  V  R  Y  Q  D
I  M  P  O  G  E  S  D  D  B  C  X  B  K  Z
P  G  O  P  T  A  T  E  E  L  L  T  J  V  R
S  R  A  E  B  N  R  S  D  S  M  B  O  T  T
Z  W  X  E  C  S  K  P  L  R  R  G  R  U  I
L  S  C  O  O  Y  Q  G  V  I  B  O  P  K  Y
S  U  X  M  H  U  J  J  G  G  B  X  S  R  K
L  V  P  D  Y  Q  Q  S  T  A  B  E  Y  O  F
S  G  U  B  Y  D  A  L  N  S  Z  D  O  O  Z
```

| | | | |
|---|---|---|---|
| Bats | Centipedes | Ladybugs | Spiders |
| Bears | Crickets | Silverfish | Swallows |

Check the answer key on page 158 to see the completed word search.

It might seem funny to name a park after the wind. That's just how **Wind Cave National Park** in South Dakota got its name. The wind makes a **whistling sound** when it moves in and out of the caves. Sometimes the wind **sucks air** into the cave, and sometimes it **blows the air out**. The way the wind moves has to do with atmospheric pressure. That is the weight of the air pressing down on the earth.

In 1881, Jesse and Tom Bingham found the entrance to **Wind Cave**. Legend tells us that the wind blowing out of the cave was **so strong** it blew Tom's hat right off. When he came back to show others, the wind had changed. This time his hat was **sucked into** the cave!

Imagine 400,000 **bats** flying out of their caves to **find dinner**. That's what happens every night at Carlsbad Caverns in New Mexico. From April to October, Brazilian free-tailed bats **gobble up insects** at sunset. Visit at the end of August and you might even see baby bats joining the party.

**QUICK QUIZ**

**Carlsbad Caverns National Park has something no other cave system has. Can you guess what it is?**

**a)** dinosaur bones

**b)** a lunchroom

**c)** a stream

**d)** an eagle's nest

Answer: b

Mammoth Cave National Park is in Kentucky. It's the longest cave system in the world. Check out some more amazing facts about this underground mystery.

Discovered: **4,000 years** ago by Native Americans

★ ★ ★

Depth: **379 feet** deep

★ ★ ★

Types of animals living in the cave: **130**

★ ★ ★

Cave temperature: **54 degrees** Fahrenheit

★ ★ ★

Visitors: **400,000 each year**

In Mammoth Cave, **lighted paths** lead the way. But you can see what it was like to explore caves before **electricity** was invented. Sign up for the Violet City Lantern Tour. You'll travel through the caves the way tourists did 200 years ago. The tour guide will give you a **kerosene lantern**. As you walk, watch your lantern cast **large shadows** on the wall.

Before **Mammoth Cave** became a national park, a man named John Croghan owned it. He was a doctor who thought that the cave air could **cure sick people**. Croghan brought some of his patients into the caves. He even set up wooden huts for them to live in. His patients kept getting sicker. The cave air didn't help at all!

Great Basin National Park in Nevada is home to **Lexington Arch**. No one is really sure how this **natural arch** got there. Some scientists think that it was once a doorway to a huge cave that mysteriously disappeared.

# HIDDEN TREASURES

Most people who visit the **Grand Canyon** come for the views. But there is a **secret** at the bottom of the canyon. Ancient **fossils of sea creatures** are buried in the limestone rock. Some of these fossils are over 1,200 million years old.

In the Grand Canyon, the **Colorado River** cuts through layers of **metamorphic rock**. This rock is called **schist**. Scientists think that the schist in the Grand Canyon is 1.75 billion years old!

Would you believe the Grand Canyon used to have a **different name**? Until 1869, it was called the "Big Canyon" or the "Great Canyon." When John Wesley Powell led the first expedition through the canyon, he saw how **beautiful** it was. That's when he changed the name!

The Grand Canyon, located in Arizona, is not the widest canyon. It's not the deepest canyon. It's not even the longest. But it is still one of the most visited canyons in the world.

The canyon is **277 miles** long.

★ ★ ★

It is **18 miles** wide at its widest point.

★ ★ ★

It is **1,800 feet** wide at its narrowest point.

It is **6,000 feet** deep.

★ ★ ★

It became a national park in **1919**.

★ ★ ★

It is considered one of the
**seven natural wonders
of the world**.

Ancient Anasazi Indians once lived in what is now **Mesa Verde National Park** in Colorado. They made their homes on **cliffs** using sandstone and adobe. Amazingly, these homes are still there! There are 600 of them. The largest is called **Cliff Palace** and has 150 rooms.

## QUICK QUIZ

Looking for adventure? You'll find it at Virgin Islands National Park. The Reef Bay Trail leads you through a thick forest and down steep slopes. At the end of the trail, you'll find rock carvings from the Taino Indians. Can you guess what these rock carvings are called?

**a)** groves

**b)** sand art

**c)** barnacles

**d)** petroglyphs

Answer: d

We all know dinosaurs are **extinct**. But did you know you can still see their **tracks** at Zion National Park in Utah? Just head over to the Dinosaur Discovery site. You'll find out all about these **giant creatures** that once roamed the earth.

Want to know what a **prehistoric camel** looked like? Visit the Badlands National Park in South Dakota. Here, you'll learn all about **ancient mammals**. You'll see the distant relatives of deer and antelope. You may even see a rhinoceros from 35 million years ago!

Long ago, Inuit lived in what is now the Gates of the Arctic National Park in Alaska. They made their **tents** out of **caribou skin** and willow trees. These tents are called *itchalik*. They could fit up to 10 people. Parts of these tents can still be seen at the park!

QUICK
QUIZ

John D. Rockefeller was a wealthy businessman who helped build roads in Acadia National Park. On many of the roads, giant rocks are used as guardrails. Some of these rocks are jagged and pointy. They have a funny nickname that honors Rockefeller. Can you guess what it is?

**a)** Rockefeller's nose

**b)** Rockefeller's teeth

**c)** Rockefeller's smile

**d)** Rockefeller's eyebrows

Answer: b

At Acadia National Park, you'll see **giant hills** made of **shells**. Some of these hills are over 30 feet high. Thousands of years ago, Native Americans left the **bones and shells of fish** in mounds. Today, these mounds give us a peek into what life was like for Native Americans all those years ago.

# Word Search

**Find the hidden treasures
of the National Parks.**

```
S N T H N D P Q Z L X P Z K O
C L C L L O S E N O B S U A H
C K A B N F O S S I L S J Q B
I A N R E B O D A U G L S M D
S L R L E R E K Y K P I L R R
N T A V B N J M I A C R L U O
I L C F I Q I K U M Y S E M Y
J I U U P N V M H X G S H M Q
A C T A Y P G E T N J Z S K L
L I T C N P W S I G U T S H H
R Y V D H S C T Q G B H O C D
U G S L P A N A F P J B E P U
S Q H X E I L A C W K N F T F
U R A S A N Y I U X V T O O I
Y D M P V Y Y T K C D L K C Q
```

Adobe    Carvings    *Itchalik*    Paintings

Bones    Fossils    Minerals    Shells

Check the answer key on page 158
to see the completed word search.

There are **fossils** of **human footprints** in Hawai'i Volcanoes National Park. Hundreds of years ago, people used to leave gifts for a goddess named Pele. In 1790, the Mount Kilauea volcano erupted. Footprints of women and children running away were left in the volcanic ash.

Pictured Rocks National Lakeshore in Michigan was named for **colors** in the **sandstone cliffs**. The rocks are mostly tan and brown. If you look closely between the layers, you can see orange, white, and black. These **colorful rocks** stretch 15 miles along Lake Superior.

# ANSWER KEY

## PAGE 61

```
X V V R B Y G P B R V I K G P
E A L D C R K Q W Y B L I C S
G K B H W G A H G B W C A W S
J C Z Z G T S F O B E R O T E
S R E W O L F D L I W D V B H
W W T J Y S Z N K X A V B T S
S A E I B Q C Y C E D D U X R
X E T Q A B W M M M G Y P M A
M X K E C B Q V J K K M P H M
H G I A R G Z X R N U D G J S
W T B J L F C R J G A G Z P R
G O A T S T A M K H U J D S E
J J M R O Y J L P E E H S N J
R D J U G D N G L K H E Z O M
O F O T U P P Q Q S X L Y W M
```

## PAGE 108

```
X J B A V H M Q S X G Q S X J
B M S T U W F T S S O Z G U E
K L A J K S R F W X O H M M Q
Y H Z O B J S U N S X R M T K
W C O H Q X E O K N W R Z G Q
C G N I L I A S Y O L D C N F
C A B D V K A P O R X N Q I I
G E N K A F V S G K K I Q F C
D N I O S Q B U N E H X D R W
N I L E L U T I L Z I W U J
O O V K M I U Z M I O A W S R
S R P I A W N M M N V X Q D H
X V A F N Y G G I G R J W Q X
S Z X C C G A C W D H I J W T
F I S H I N G K S J I Y A I K
```

## PAGE 133

```
C K M Q Y Z G T L A T A T S E
N E S I L V E R F I S H W F R
C U N J R S T R P L G A J Y L
N R V T D Q C C M I L W N O F
X L I X I B A G Y L V S J P F
F Y Z C W P D B O M P G R K R
B H U D K H E W C I V R Y Q D
I M P O G E S D D B C X B K Z
P G O P T A T E L L T J V R
S R A E B N R S D S M B O T T
Z W X E C S K P L R R G R U I
L S C O O Y Q G V I B O P K Y
S U X M H U J J G G B X S R K
L V P D Y Q Q S T A B E Y O F
S G U B Y D A L N S Z D O O Z
```

## PAGE 155

```
S N T H N D P Q Z L X P Z K O
C L C L L O S E N O B S U A H
C K A B N F O S S I L S J Q B
I A N R E B O D A U G L S M D
S L R L E R E K Y K P I L R R
N T A V B N J M I A C R L U O
I L C F I Q I K U M Y S E M Y
J I U U P N V M H X G S H M Q
A C T A Y P G E T N J Z S K L
L I T C N P W S I G U T S H H
R Y V D H S C T Q G B H O C D
U G S L P A N A F P J B E P U
S Q H X E I L A C W K N F T F
U R A S A N Y I U X V T O O I
Y D M P V Y Y T K C D L K C Q
```

We hope you enjoyed this brief tour through the secrets and highlights of the national parks. While we've packed the book with information, there is so much more for you to discover. So start exploring and compiling secrets of your own!

If you enjoyed *Secrets of the National Parks*, check out *Secrets of Our Nation's Capital, Secrets of Disneyland,* and *Secrets of Walt Disney World*!

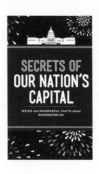

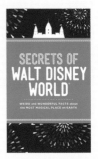